Reflective Mind

MICHAEL J GARDNER

AKA THE WALKING POET

To DIANE

BEST WISHES

M. J. Gardner

AKA THE WALKING POET

16/11/23

FIRST EDITION
Published in 2023 by
GREEN CAT BOOKS
19 St Christopher's Way
Pride Park
Derby
DE24 8JY
www.green-cat.shop

ISBN: 978-1-913794-48-4

Poem for Frances

A rose by any other name would surely be as sweet,
But I find your perfume is really hard to beat.
And as I run my fingers through your hair, so soft it is,
And gentle to the touch. It's then I feel the love within,
The love that excites my heart and fills my life so much.

The love for you that doth my heart entwine, I put in
words
So you can see how much you really mean to me.
I hear your voice float so gentle on the breeze,
it whispers softly like the trees. And like the trees, your
Voice doth speak to me of love, and I thank,
With all my heart, my Lord above.

My darling Frances, this gift of love that we do share,
I put in rhyme that you may see the love there.
There within my heart, so strong and true,
This love that burns so bright for you.

This love that doth my life enhances,
I give to you, my darling Frances.

*Both the book and poem are in memory of my Vera
Frances.*

CONTENTS

Acknowledgements

Thank you to Headway for being there when my wife had brain haemorrhage in 2018.

And to the District Nurses who helped Frances with palliative care in 2021.

And to my doctor and my Social Prescriptive Link Worker who helped me through my grief, and to all in the walking groups I lead for their friendship and support.

Part One

Headway

Challenge for Headway

Headway have challenges for you to take, and through the effort that you make, in sponsorship new funds to give,
So those who suffer, with new encouragement and hope can live.

To help those who from head injury suffer, and support their father, son, daughter and mother,
Through their anxiety and pain.
To guide and help new life to gain.

If you can, take a challenge, show your skill. Show to others it is your will, to help those who suffer pain and stress,
And bring hope to mind, so they worry less.

Help Headway support folks through anxiety and pain. That after injury confidence and new life may gain.

Headway was There by Their Side

When a friend sustained an ABI, Headway was there by their side.
They gave encouragement and hope, and showed them a new way in life to cope.

And through their kindness and compassion,
Helped my friend to build confidence in a new life to fashion.

Through rehabilitation and learning skills,
My friend regained independence and shared many thrills.

Having seen the difference Headway made,
My friend would not their kindness and compassion trade.

If you have a friend who suffers so,
Tell them of Headway, so that Headway's kindness and support they can know.

Hope is Headway

When my wife suffered an ABI,
It broke my heart and made me cry.

As she laid there so ill in bed,
The docs and nurses to her head did care.
My heart was full of fear and dread.

But then Headway came their support to share,
It helped to put my fear to bed.

The support of Headway helped us, this painful time to
get through.

And helped us to move on, our hope and confidence to
renew.

So to Headway we say thanks a lot.
Forget what you did for us, we will not.

For the encouragement and hope you give,
In helping folks to a new way of life to live.

Ode to Headway

I write this to say thanks to Headway.
The support they gave my wife and me, I remember
every day.

Their volunteer that came was so caring and so kind.
The compassion and help she gave to us, no better could
I find.

If a head injury you have, or it is from which you
recover,
Headway is there for you, to give help and support to
get you through.

The help they give is like no other, their kindness and
compassion can ease the stress you suffer.

All this I write from experience, of what they did for
me and my wife,

Their kindness, care and compassion helped us both to
build a new life.

Part Two

Grief & Compassion

Legacy Fulfilled

Now my princess has passed away,
I am again on my own, and long for her love with me
to stay.

I seek for her legacy of kindness to live on,
So that through the love she left with me,
the fruits of her legacy continue to be.
And so to others her kindness share,
Even though she is not there.

I walk with this quest on my own.
I shut my door and to loneliness once more am prone.

Friends, please, with love and compassion gather
round.
Help, support me through my pain, so that I can her
legacy fulfill and see again.

She is There Each and Every Morning

She is there each and every morning, as I hear the birds sing as the day is dawning.

She is there as breakfast I make, and in every sip of tea I take.

She is there as I walk along the street, and Amongst the friends I go to meet.

My princess is there every day, as I journey along life's lonely way.

And as I lay my head down to sleep, my heart aches and I begin to weep.

In the loneliness of my room, I feel the pain, And cry myself to sleep again.

Legacy of Love

This legacy of love that within my heart dost live,
That I, even in my grief, seek new ways to give.

And as I, in remembrance of my princess, live,
To reflect the kindness and compassion, and care for
folks; that was her passion.

So through friendship, and poetry,
I can express the love she left for me.

Lost Memories

I wake each day, and the darkest mist do find
That my friends and family are hidden there, behind
Memories of their kindness, and their love is lost to me.

Somewhere in the deepest cavern of my mind,
A longing for such love you may find.

Perhaps the sound of music will help me to
Some memory reclaim,
And in those precious moments, love of family share
again.

The Mind, a Treasured Gift

The mind is such a treasured gift,
From where memories of joy and love we lift.

Pain and fear we seek to leave behind, for they bring
such stress to heart and mind.

But the memories we treasure above all others,
Are of the love from brothers, sisters, fathers and
mothers.

And when we fall in love, a joyous blessing to our heart.
Memories such as this are life's treasure from which we
never want to part.

But sadly, dementia comes and robs us of these
precious thoughts.
But through kind words and music sound,

Some memory recall can be found.
And in those moments so precious, and perhaps so rare,
Love of family we can, in those moments share.

Charlotte

I am blest by a social prescriptive worker,
Her name is Charlotte, she's very kind and so caring.

In my time of grief and pain,
She, with words of tenderness and care, from the
darkness helped me lift my head again.

She helps and encourages me a future and way of life to
see.
She tells me my poems I should publish.

So I write this one for you, so you know
How much I, and others cherish you.

<u>Ode to Brocks Hill Walking Group</u>

We walk upon Brocks Hill land
And join together for a walk,
Engrossed in conversation talk.
Some walk fast and some walk slow,

Does not matter, we do not care,
It is exercise and friendship
In which we seek to share.

Bright and Joyous Morn

I awake to a bright and joyous morn,
As the sun, in all its glorious beauty dawn.

As it rises above the trees, and glistens through the
wafting leafs.

The birds bob across the ground, and bees as they
pollinate the flowers, make their gentle buzzing sound.

Squirrels scamper out of sight, and crack the nuts with
all their might.

Then as the dusk begins to fall, I take my rest within
my chair, and with my friend that beauty share.

As such beauty I recall, so moved am I, I begin to
weep.
And so I gently fall asleep.

The Sun, it Shines So Bright Today

The sun, it shines so bright today.
As I walk so quietly on my way, through the woods
beneath the trees,
I feel the soft and gentle breeze upon my face, from
whence it comes, I cannot trace.

As I come out of the woods to a field so wide, I am
filled with such pride, and gaze upon the beauty of the
valleys and the hills, that challenges my walking skills.

I come to my village, my home once more. I sit with a
drink, and as I reflect and think upon the beauty that
I've seen once more; such beauty in my heart and mind
I store.

The Comfort of Nature

As I sit on this bench and look upon the pond,
And take in the beauty that I see, that doth lift my
spirits and bring such glee.

I see the rushes and the reeds, and look up at the
shading trees.
I hear the birds as they sing and land upon each
branch.

It is so calming and serene, it puts me in a trance.
And as I get up to walk, I look into the pond, and the
water lilies in all their beauty glance.

And as I make my way back to the bench, I the
comforting arm of nature sense,
And seek within its hold to dwell, and see such beauty of
which no words can adequately tell.

As I Wake Up to Each New Day

As I wake up to each new day,
I ask myself, who will be my guide and show the way?
Through my fear and painful grief,
Who will dry my falling tears, and through their
kindness bring relief?

Who is going to love me now
And wipe and soothe my troubled brow?
And when the pain of grief comes again, show me love
to ease my pain?

There is only one I really know,
And with His love and strength I seek to grow.
Christ speaks to me, in truth, He says,
I am with you through all your days.

Day by Day

Day by day we fuss and stress, reach for things we
cannot get.
Our heart and mind do take the strain and we feel such
a mess.
There is a way to help the heart and the mind refresh.
Walking is good for you in so many ways and helps to
relieve the stress.
In walking groups, you will find new friends as you
walk among the trees and fields,
As such beauty and fresh air washes all around, it is
there a sense of peace is found,
stride out in confidence, enjoy the flowers, fields and
trees,
and give your heart, your mind the care they need.

All I Can Say

I walk around the town and country park.
"'Tis healthy for me," are the words I so often hark.

Walking is like gold for the heart and mind,
And as I lay there in my bed, I get a poetic thought
within my head.

I think of all the friends I've made, and all the kind
words that have been said.

With this in mind, I joyfully go and do my part, and
lead others on the way; and tell them, "Walking is good
for you,", What more can I say?

Wellbeing for Heart and Mind

For your wellbeing, don't be shy, stagnate, or let life go by.
Come with us and take a walk.

And as we tread along our way, in conversation talk.
And when our walk, it doth end,
You will find you've made a friend.

In walking and friendship with us, you will find
The benefits to both your heart and mind.

As I Journey Through Each Day

As I journey through each day,
My part in life I seek to play.
As I lead the group on a walk,
And share in friendship as we talk.
And as I continue through the week,
Showing kindness and compassion in all I speak.

Holding out a caring hand to those in need,
So that such compassion, some healing for their pain
doth feed.

And as the month I journey through,
Dear friends, it's kindness and care I offer you.

To be there in your stress and pain,
To give encouragement and hope,
So that you can find new ways to cope.

And so each day these gifts I give,
So you all in friendship and support may live.

Bank Holiday Walk

I walk lonely down the cut, carefully treading along the path,
Dodging every branch and rut.

I watch a dog play in the water, his antics make me laugh.
I met a man and his daughter; their barge was so long but shallow in its draught.

I see the water lilies and their pads giving shade to the fishes.
I hope none are ever caught and end on people's dishes.

All this happened on Bank Holiday Monday.
There was no wellbeing walk that day,
I walked alone along the way.
So all this I share with you,

It's not the same without the group, that's all that I can say.
I wish you were all there too.

As I Walk Along a Lonely Street

As I walk along a lonely street,
The beauty of the rising dawn I meet.
In the sunlight, the beauty of the flowers begins to
shine,
And brings such warmth and blessing to this heart of
mine.

As I turn into the park
I see dogs play,
and hear them bark.
Leaves whisper gently in the breeze,
As I slowly walk beneath the majestic trees.

The birds sing their song, some so sweetly soft,
some so definitely loud,
And all as they glide beneath a floating cotton cloud.

And as I walk upon the grass,
A squirrel in a hurry doth dane to pass.
As the sun continues to rise and shine.
It reminds me of the resurrection
of this Lord of mine.

Exciting Walk

Very exciting to see and learn
About the badgers, trees and fields.

And share in the beauty that they yield,
'Tis a joy upon the mind,
To be in nature,
And in friendship so beautifully kind.

Healing for the Heart

I walk alongside a babbling brook,
And watch tadpoles seek a home,
To shelter from the midday sun.
I too search for respite from the heat.

So I go to the woods, where cooler air I meet
Beneath the canopy of trees,
And as the air flows past the leaves,
and causes them to rustle on the breeze,

I hear a blackbird sing his song,
It lifts my spirit to carry on.
Through the woods and across the stream,
So wonderful it is to dream,
And like a healing to my heart,
It helps me from my grief and sadness part.

Take Your Heart for a Walk

Day by day we fuss and stress, reaching for things we
cannot get.
Our heart and mind do take the strain, and we feel such
a mess.
There is a way to help the heart and the mind refresh.
Walking is good for you in so many ways, and helps to
relieve the stress.

In walking groups, you will find new friends, as you
walk among the trees and fields.
As such beauty and fresh air washes all around, it is
where a sense of peace is found.
So stride out in confidence, enjoy the flowers, fields and
trees, and give your heart, your mind, the care they
really need.

If You Struggle with Loneliness or Grief

If you struggle with loneliness or grief,
Please don't let it bring you down, or shatter your belief.
Reach out, for there are folks who care, who seek to help and bring relief.

I know what it's like to suffer so, in life to live, or which way to go. I did not have a clue.
This message to you I give, a message I have embraced,
It gave hope to me, so that now my life doth grow.

I joined a group of walkers, who gave support and care to me.
Their friendship helped me so.
Walking is good for the heart and mind.

Friendship helps ease my grief and loneliness,
and in its place compassion I do find.
Let people help, don't push them away,
Let them, in friendship help today.

Terror and Turmoil

Today I woke up to find
Terror and turmoil troubling my mind.
Wanting to give up, wanting to fight.
Not knowing which one was going to be right.

Frightened to lose the ground I had to gain,
Frightened to relive the heartache and hurt that to my
heart had coursed pain.

So to the Salvation Army, off I did go.
I found two nice ladies, whose kind words healing did
sow.
To them I say thank you for the kindness they gave,
That I can move on from the fear, and my confidence
save.

Get Involved

Sport is good for the body and the mind,
And if you get involved, new friends you'll find.
So get off the couch, forget the videos, buttons and the switches,
Play your sports on real pitches.

Whether you be boy or girl, get out there and give it a whirl.
You could become a Lineker or Lucy Bronze. Give your best and play the game of which you're fond.

Ode to Menphys Café

I sit within the Menphys Café
Enjoying a morning latte.
I hear conversations all around,
Amid the smiles and friendships found.

Behind all this there is a course
To help children in their need,
To get them from their pain,
Stress and discomfort freed.

Help a Child Today

Each time I come into the Menphys Café,
They give a smile that brings such joy, and are so kind
As they seek to help each girl and boy,
To raise the funds to support each child, who struggles
with physical pain or a troubled mind.

If such a child were ours today,
We would seek help and find a way,
To bring healing to the body, and
Peace to mind.

So with your heart, please be.
Give what you can to help a child,
And put upon their face a lovely smile.

I Want to Sing my Song

In the subconscious of my mind, there are songs that
the conscious cannot find.
Then my family comes to visit me, play some music and
set them free.

As the music it doth start,
My subconscious plays its part.
And as the tunes and words come to the fore,
I find that I can sing once more.

But when the music ends,
Then my mind, the songs, back to the subconscious
sends.

Please continue with research to find,
Music's influence on the mind.
I want to love my family and sing my song,
And return them to the conscious where they belong.

I am Captured by this Beast

I am captured by this beast, it pulls my memories out of
reach,
It robs me of memories of family and friends,
And its cruelty to me never ends.

No one is safe from its hold,
Because it will attack both young and old.
But there is hope, for music has, it seems, to have some
influence on the mind.
And bring musical memories to the fore,
So I, with my family can share familiar songs once
more.

So please support the Dementia Choir
To fulfill their desire
for more funding and research in music therapy,
To bring some hope, some joy to them and me.

In the Event, Help Dementia UK

Dementia comes and robs the mind,
And makes it hard memories of family and friends to
find.

If you can, in an event take part, and with a kind and
caring heart, raise the funds that we do need,
Help us, our outreach to seed.

To reach more patients and their family,
And from their isolation free.
And give reassurance that they're not alone,
And don't need to make the journey on their own.

Part Three

Faith

Ode to Wigston Magna Methodist Church

When invited to be a member
Of my local church,
I joyfully accepted,

For they to me have been a lifeline, as I to loss of wife
adapted, they came with kindness and compassion.
They did not leave me in the lurch,

But lifted me with Christ-like love, gave me hope, a
new life to fashion.

And now I seek to take my place, to do the same for
others, within the mission of this church, and with the
fellowship as they in worship gathers, join in Christ, with
my sisters and my brothers.

There is a Place

There is a place before the cross, where we bring our shame and our loss,
And as we look at Christ's face, we see His smile of love, as He shows a forgiving grace.

When the loss of loved one we do grieve,
His love, comfort we receive.
He helps us through our heartache and our pain,
He guides us, a new life to gain.

So as you stand in that place of sanctuary, and feel that you are on your own,
Remember you are not alone.
For through the cross, you will see
His love is there for you and me.

At Easter Time

At Easter time, as we see the crucifixion cross,
We are reminded of the pain, humiliation, and
remember how Christ died. And we feel the loss.

And in those days, as folks looked on, some in fear,
And with Christ's mother, shed a tear.

His blood was shed to cleanse our soul, His body, in
communion makes us whole.
The tomb is cold and empty now,
Because before our risen Lord we bow.

The Lord is with us, as from the grave He lives again,
And comes to ease our grief and pain.
And as His glory shines through our hearts' open door,
He lives within our hearts, and gives His love, hope
and peace once more.

Christmas Has Come

Christmas has come and brings such joy,
Especially for each girl and boy,
But for some it's loneliness and loss that is their pain.

Through loss of family, or husband, or wife, it impacts
upon their life.
Lonely or grieving and all alone,
No one to love them, and they're on their own.

Let's all reach out with joy and compassion,
And help those in loneliness or grief,
A new life to fashion.
And in friendship ease their pain,
So they can share the joy of Christmas once again.

Christmas: The Birth of a Special Child

At Christmas we celebrate the birth of a special child,
As he lays in a manger there, ever so meek and mild.

As they saw a distant light shining there, o' so bright,
that was a special star,
Three wise men travelled from distant lands, that were
away so far.

They came to see this special baby boy,
God's son, who came into the world to bring much hope
and joy.

And as they gave their gifts of gold, frankincense and
myrrh,
They knelt in awe and wonder, as they saw the Christ
child laying there.

And so let us be like the wise men, and bring our gifts,
our gifts of praise and love,
And as we gaze upon the Christ child, give thanks to
our God above.

I Look at the Cross Upon the Table

I look at the cross upon the table,
and am reminded of Christ's love.
And through His spirit I am able,
To serve and bring hope like the dove.

And like a dove, the Word of God from which I
speak, will land upon a distant peak,
And guide you from the valley of fear,
And give you the encouragement and hope you seek.

You do not travel all alone, be assured the Lord is
here.
There may be only one set of footprints on the road,
That's because the Lord carries you, and your load.
And knowing this within your soul, walk with confidence
towards your goal.

Imagine if you Could Hold the Christ Child

Imagine if you could hold the Christ child,
And he lay in your arms so meek and mild.
And as you embrace him to your breast,
Your heart, so full of love, races within your chest.

And as you bow to lay him down to sleep,
With a heart so full, tears of love and joy you weep.

He lays in the manger so quiet now,
To love him forever is your vow.
So embrace the love that he gives,
For in your heart He always lives.

Part Four

Reflections

Both Heat and Drought

Once more we face both heat and drought.
People struggle to find supply,
As flowers and fields continue to fry.

Animals too, they do suffer from a lack of water.
Cats and dogs struggle too, because they can't go out in
the heat and relieve themselves as they usually do.

Some sick and elderly have no supply, and bottled water
they need to buy.
They cannot get out to the shop,
Because the heat is so hot.

So to all let's be kind,
And be careful with the water that we use,
And our supply not abuse.

Folks Suffer and Fields Bake

Amid the recent heat and humidity, folks suffer and
fields bake.
Fires burned. No trains stopped people's mobility.
A danger to people's lives did make.
People now a word of thanks do say,
As fresher air comes their way, giving hope for a cooler
day.

Looking forward to the rain, to feed the land and ease
the pain.
And as we go upon our way, let's not take for granted
wind, sun and rain.
And seek to heal the climate change, so this doesn't
happen again.

This Tragedy is No Fun

People struggle with the prices and can't afford to use their kitchen devices.

Food gets short because of drought and heat. Folk are struggling their bills to meet.

So to the food banks they do go.
Some feel so ashamed, they don't want other folks to know.

Government needs to solve this problem quick,
Before people become unwell and seriously sick.
Something needs to be done,
Because this tragedy is no fun.

Wildlife Suffer Too

Amidst this time of heat and lack of rain,
The wildlife, too, feel the pain.
Through lack of food and lack of water,

In their weakness they can't move like they oughta.
They get tired and down do lay. And so become in
weakness prone to prey.

So take care of wildlife,
For the animals and birds, put some water in a tray.

The Beauty of the Day

I look out of my window square and look upon the trees, and the clouds above that float so gently on the breeze.

The leaves waft and branches bend in majesty,
As if they know the beauty of the flowers that blossom down below.

That with their colours show a glorious view and brings to me a smile,
So seeing all of this from my window square, I linger for a while.

And as I journey through the day, I seek to do the same,
And put a smile upon your face, through everything I say.

I Saw a Picture of a Man

I saw a picture of a man, his head within his hands,
And on his face, a look of doom.
And with a heart that was so full of gloom,
He said, "I feel the heartache and the pain,"
And then he prays for some hope and peace to gain.
If he's your friend in despair, will you stay, and help,
and care?

Ode to Ross

Ross, this week, was not well,
So could not his jokes and stories tell.

We enjoy his joyous and cheery chatter,
It helps make our troubles seem not to matter.

So, Ross, we wish you well,
And soon be back, your jokes and stories once again to tell.

Dear Queen Elizabeth, as you Heavenward Depart

Dear Queen Elizabeth, as you heavenward depart,
To you, our love we give from within a broken heart.

It is with such sorrow and such pain,
We walk in hope that in Heaven we will meet again.

You were the rock within our nation,
Your service you did without hesitation.

To the people of the Commonwealth was kind,
A monarch with greater compassion you could not find.

And now as you leave this world,
Words of love and condolences from our hearts
unfurled.

And as you peacefully leave us now, before you,
Ma'am, we give one last respectful bow.

Truly Empty Space

Folks line up along a tree-lined street,
Waiting patiently the Queen's coffin to greet.
Some bow their head, some cry a tear,
To some the loss of our Queen is hard to bear.

As the cortege comes along, the King in his pain
endeavours to be strong.
At Westminster Hall the Queen lies majestically in
state,
The crowd come and bow, then pass at a respectful
rate.

On Monday, our Queen will be at last laid in her
resting place,
For those who lived within her reign, there will forever
be a truly empty space.

Seek a Song

The melody of life reflects our mood in different ways,
as we in life on our journey go.
Sometimes it's loud, and a crescendo doth make,
As our life, like a raging river of stress and pain doth
flow.

And when in a peaceful, loving mind, life's river flows
so smoothly that we a sense of peace we do find.

And so in life, seek a song, a song of love and kindness
too, For all who truly care for you,
And to all, from your heart, kindness and compassion to
impart.

Time is Such an Elusive Thing

Time is such an elusive thing.
Sometimes it's slow and sometimes fast; those precious
moments don't seem to last.

From time of birth, great joy it brings, and in time of
death the sounds of remembrance into eternity rings.

My life has been written in the book of time, but none of
it can I claim as really mine. Each moment that we
enjoy drifts into history, and becomes precious memories
for you and me.

Take each precious moment and lock it in your heart, so
that each moment becomes like a pearl of which you'll
never part.

Exercise and Wellbeing

Oadby, Wigston Activ arrange exercise and sport.
All to keep you healthy and mobile in the way you
sought.

They arrange walks, sports and all kinds of matches,
So there is so much to choose, whatever your fancy
catches.

Come along and make your choice,
Or even volunteer and to others show the way.
Promote healthy exercise and wellbeing to folks today.

And through sports, and walks, and play,
We help them a healthy life to live.
Of all the gifts in all the world, this is the best gift that
we could ever give.

Jousting Knights

I went to Never Castle to see the jousting knights,
And watch them fight with lance and horse,
As they go charging down the course.

A lethal blow to inflict, and knock each other to the
ground.
Suddenly, the lance strikes the red knight,
It makes a lethal blow upon his chest.

Blue knight celebrates and claims to be the best.
Then the red knight gets up, draws his sword,
And gives a shout, "Come and fight!
Your sword play to test."

They swung their swords, which was such a feat,
As each sought the other one to beat.
Blue knight had one more swing.

Red knight in pain, hit the dust. But got up again,
And thrust his sword in the blue knight's side,
And struck him down. The red knight had won the
battle,
And beat his foe.
So to claim his crown did go.

Joy of the Garden Centre

Today I have come to the garden centre, to look for outdoor tables for the folks of Beech Court.

As I searched, I could not find the style I had in mind,
There nothing, no not nought, that fitted the brief, or could be bought.

But I continued to walk around, looking at bushes, trees and flowers.
Such beauty, joy within my
Heart and soul, it showers.

So if you are down and feeling low, off to a garden centre go. Share in the beauty of flowering plants,
And experience the joy and peace it grants.

Off we Go to The Supermarket

Off we go to the supermarket,
In the car seeking a space to park it.
And as we walk up and down each aisle,
Occasionally we stop and pause awhile.

Try to choose the right Christmas fayre,
Remembering what our friends like and in which they
would share,
Looking for ingredients for a Christmas cake,
And for the icing for decoration to make.

And as we make our way home,
A friend calls us on the phone.
It's the words that we most fear,
They say sorry, we can't make it this year.
What do I do with all this food?
I simply lost my festive mood.

Part Five

Family &
Friendship

Family Love is my Treasure

Today I get into my car,
With a plan to travel far.
Down to Surrey is where I go.
Precious time with family to know.

Now on my own I do treasure,
Time with family without measure.
Without their care, love, support,
I don't think I would have found the peace that for
long I sought.

And now with their love I am able
To build a life that is strong and stable.
So this rhyme I write so you can see how much family
really means to me.

Friendship at the Centre of Life

Friendship is at the centre of life. Friends become husbands,
Friends become wives,
Friends are there for us, in the joy and the pain.

With friendships in our lives, a richness we gain.
True friendship is intreasure in our lives,
Whether with neighbours, sons or daughters, or husbands and wives.

Friendship is the gem that brings richness to lives, giving without wanting, kindness and compassion. These virtues we learn, and we grow,
So that, in our lives, friendship is what we sow.

Friendship Fills Our Heart

As we walk along the busy street, and once again our
group of friends to meet,
We turn into a leafy lane and a view of nature gain.

And as we travel across the park, we see dogs play,
and hear their bark.
We hear the birds in the trees, and watch as they take
flight upon the breeze.

'Tis a joy as they sing out loud and glide below the
drifting cloud.
And as a sense of friendship fills our heart, a blessing
from which we will not part.

Exercise is good for both heart and mind, but it is within
the gift of friendship that we find kindness and support
that is given beyond all measure. And is what we truly
treasure.

This is why each week we meet, because exercise and
friendship is what we seek,
And to help and support one another as if we were
sister, brother.

Ode to Claire

There is a lady that I know,
So kind and caring, through and through.
She celebrates her birthday, fifty, so they say,
But she looks like twenty-five, as she is full of jollity
and life.
So Claire, we all wish you a happy birthday,
And lots of best wishes and love come your way.

It's Kindness that Matters

What do I look like today?
Am I fat or am I thin?
Am I short or am I tall?

Does it really matter at all?
Do folk really care,
Or is it in your personality,
Your kindness and compassion,
Those things that come from the heart, that folks really
need to share?

If you have a heart of gold,
Full of kindness and compassion, you'll stand tall in all
the world,
No matter what the fashion.

My Loved One's Love for Me Does No Longer Flow

My loved one's love for me does no longer flow,
For family and me she seems not to know.
Dementia has come and robbed her of love and family.
It really is so sad for me to see.

She is now like a shadow of herself,
For she cannot show the care and kindness that was her wealth.
I come in love because I care,
but it feels like I'm not there.

I hear that music can influence the mind,
And help memories of songs to find.
My hope is that this therapy gains support,
So that family and loved ones can be united like we aught.

About the Author

Let me introduce myself, I'm Michael J Gardner Aka The Walking Poet. Why the Walking Poet you ask. Well I am a volunteer wellbeing walk leader for my local borough council. But when I started with the group I was prescribed to it by a Social Prescriptive Link Worker after my wife died. The group was the best place for me, they helped a lot.

When I was working I was a safety rep, and when I was mid sixty's I trained as a Lay Preacher, my poems are written in the way they are because I write what I feel. And writing that way these poems I share with you have been a good therapy to get me through my grief. I am now a Volunteer for Leicestershire, Leicester and Rutland Headway, and that is why I have put a donation link below.

Ways to Donate to Leicestershire Leicester and Rutland Headway

Through their website

www.headwayleicester.org.uk – click on the donate button in the top right corner.

Through JustGiving

www.justgiving.com/headwayleicester - Click on the donate button.

Through Caf online

www.cafonline.org – Search for us using our charity Number: 1074011

For more information about our books and publishing services, please visit

www.green-cat.shop

Printed in Great Britain
by Amazon

27172333R00047